RAW ~~FLESH~~ FLASH
THE INCOMPLETE, UNFINISHED DOCUMENTING OF

POETRY BY

DONOVAN HUFNAGLE

UnCollected Press

RAW ~~FLESH~~ FLASH
THE INCOMPLETE, UNFINISHED DOCUMENTING OF
Copyright © 2022 by DONOVAN HUFNAGLE

Cover Art by Ezekiel Wizell

Book Design by:

UnCollected Press
8320 Main Street, 2nd Floor
Ellicott City, MD 21043

For more books by UnCollected Press:
www.therawartreview.com

First Edition 2022
ISBN: 979-8-9867243-4-8

This book inhales the wind of collaboration. I want to thank many such as the interview contributors, the several tattoo shops, the artists, Virtuoso Tattoo, Deso, EZ, my family, Lunk, tattoos in general, and the many more I didn't mention here.

I dedicate the book to my wife and three children.

The support, encouragement, and final approval from my wife are crucial. The constant love is even more so. When she gives the green light, I know I have a winning poem. Without my three children, the book may not be here. Kali, thank you for "Confuzzled"; Sebastian, thank you for your overall inspiration, especially for "The Burn"; and Nayeli, thank you for "Unicorn Tattoo."

THE ~~FLASH~~ FLESH

SECTION 44-34-10 (4)

TO AMEND TITLE 44 OF THE CODE OF LAWS ███████ ████████████, BY ADDING CHAPTER 34, TO PROVIDE FOR THE STANDARDS, REQUIREMENTS, AND PROCEDURES OF TATTOOING CERTAIN PERSONS UNDER CERTAIN CONDITIONS AND AT CERTAIN LOCATIONS; ████████████████████████████, TO PROVIDE THAT IT IS UNLAWFUL TO TATTOO ANOTHER PERSON UNLESS THE TATTOO ARTIST MEETS THE REQUIREMENTS OF CHAPTER 34 OF TITLE 44.

SECTION 44-34-10 (3)
'Tattoo artist' means a person who practices body tattooing and who meets the requirements of this chapter.

I Tell Them Ink is Mightier Than Pen and Sword

The most common question is—*will it hurt*? I want to say, *fuck yeah*
it hurts. There will be a stainless steel needle climbing into you—
ink eats your flesh away. I cut and burn you.

Scarred!

Motherfucker!

For Life!

I want to say this, but I don't.
I want to say this, but instead I say it depends on where you get it:

I point to the ankle if she wants her dragonfly to strike
the bicep. The ankle hurts more because it scratches bone.

I point to the calf if he wants Spiderman to spin a web
on the ankle. The calf hurts more because it vampires
the muscle.

I point to the ribs if he wants tiger claws to scratch down
his shoulder blade. The ribs hurt more because it beats
on your heart.

I point to the wrist when she wants her lily pad to rest
on the foot. The wrist hurts more because the veins kiss
the skin.

I want to say it hurts everywhere:
The pulse from the vibrating gun in my hand;
the Hydrocodone I take each morning just to hunch over
another thigh for five hours;
The disappointment in my mother's eyes.

If you ask anyone who has tattoos, they will say—
yes, it hurts—not that bad, though. It is bearable.
Tolerable. They laugh at the girl crying,

1

lying on a massage table, on her side as I stroke my
vibrating pen (in this case sword) down her thigh. She stops mid
line.

It is like one of the deepest secrets in life.
Santa Clause. The Tooth Fairy. And Tattoos
don't hurt—that bad. And, of course, when you look
to the left, you see a woman holstering a revolver. The tip
just peeks from under her shorts.

When you look to the right, you see a man anchored to a ship
on his forearm. The ocean splashes your cheek.

When you look straight into that mirror, you see a blank canvas
wanting. Your mind knows—no
but the reflection of your eyes want—yes.

You ask—*Will it hurt*? I want to say—*Yes*, your father's anger
when he says—*you are dumber than I thought*—he pulls
your collar down just past the tip of the winged gargoyle;
your guilt from hiding your first tattoo from your father for two
years; and your mother's disappointment,
in her eyes, when your father speaks to her that way.

Just yesterday, I wanted four little letters tattooed on my
wrist: Lunk

L

U

N

K

a nickname for my best friend. When the ink crawled like black beetles down the first line, I cried. It was like I was visiting him in the hospital after months of chemo, which failed to kill the monster in his chest.

When you die, haunt me—I said. *It hurts*—is what I wanted to say.

1. describe your tat   RAkers old Font, 5 Letters words
Steed out, From other languages, Bertha meanian
2. why did you decide on the location of the tat?
not visible all time, on arms.
3. what was your original idea for the tat?
Something meaning ful
4. did it turn out as you hoped why or why not? turned out as he wanted simples, mission accomplished.
5. whats the meaning of your tat?
Journey, life.
6. what shop and srtist did the ink work for you? Diff places, wanted new experience.
7. how often do people notice your tat or comment about it?
If thes comfy or vorked with, others dont NBd.
8. what do they say? Judged), thinks hes cool.
9. have you ever been discrimintaed against about your ink work, example would be a job that requires all tats to be covered or a person would date you etc for it. maybe they judged you for them?
Mom hates tattoos. threatened kick him out.
, wears sleeves to cover.
So the fun part lol Tell me anything about your life going on when you got it how you felt what it meant or didnt what it means now or what you think about it now would you change it? it can be as long or short as you want.

Wanted private meanings.

Aristotle Principle He wants te stick with soul.
Defines Person Has purpose. tyks, Felm.
tAles what your here fer. Knew it has his purpse
to gain knowledge, Live with purpose. *get lost
in the purpose. Bud - safer - in sandscrit means
Journey. Always Appreciate the Journey.

4

Cam Christy Lockwood - hip tape.
6-B - Rebirth. new Begings. New BaBy. new chapter
after drug addictions. daughters 8 now. 36cm3/403
and tats. Maybe more feathers. - different lifestyle.
goals to well towards onestful. 3 Years of
Change.   ncones totally aware of the Ink
tape Fuck Point. Nottedo fer sale. newBegins,
daughters Initals on shoulders.
7-B ∕ Butterflys. Fly at 9 xe Acessback.
stages in life. expanded. 8yrold now.

5

Cover Up

He says that our minds don't fully
mature until age 25—
Glenlivet, Goat Gouda, Shade
Trees, Monopoly.

So was I aware at sixteen, while
my bare chest pickled
on the plastic-wrapped-
pleather barber's chair while
the needle ripped into my baby
backs?

10 years later the dragon
is calf brains and tongue
sautéed with scrambled eggs.

The earth rests
on discolored moles and is now
a rubber bouncy-ball my five-year-old rescued
from the cage located in the middle
of Albertsons. It meowed to her. It purred.
She had to have it. It was neglected.

How did I stand
watch over myself
at sixteen?

The lines on my back
are "blown out." He says.
The "black is mute." The "scales blend"
together like double boiling chocolate chips.
"Can my daughter
become the dragon?" I ask.

Confuzzled

When my gargoyle was sewn back together
cross-eyed, I could not
put all the pieces back together again.

The doctor says he tries his best to puzzle
the tattoo straight, but the black
and gray blurred into the canvas.

The question, then, is
if he will ever be able to look
into my eyes again—the doctor,
not the gargoyle.

Should I ask
my tattoo artist to stare
into his eyes—the gargoyle,
not the doctor?—question why yolk
continues to spoil from my wound?

Should I admire the scar, the mound of skin
that dams the two sides of stale ink?

Does it now belong to Dr. Frankenstein? Golem
molded new?

If these are the questions to ask, the question to ask next, then, is
if possession is nine-tenths of the law,

                    1878-Preacher Anderson Hatfield chose
                    that the hogs stay with the possessor.

                    1901-McCoy and Hatfield still feud

1998-984 S.W.2d 344

Garza court found possession trumps
the claim of a party who has neither record
title nor possession, mere possession is
subordinate to the claims of a party having
record title to the property,

whose fractured tattoo weeps on my arm?

When I say I am a Samurai

I lie.

I almost faint to a sword ripping the stomach's
flesh in a Kung Fu flick.

I almost faint to the *Shīwàng*
glazed with my sweat on your back;

Hope is swallowed by a Venus Flytrap
in the shape of your mouth

I see images of death, and
I've never even been to Japan.

Diego

…out for a cigarette, coffee, and tattoo.
Numb, dangled over the chair arm,
the right foot asks, "will it hurt?"
The left waits like Mother.

"Only when wearing shoes." The puncturing needle replies.

Orange bleeds into blood like a painter's tablet
of sunset. The sun burns his veins.
And his 26 bones (~~28 if you include the sesamoid~~) ache.

"Does the sun shine, yet?" the right foot asks.

"bzzzzzzzzzzzzz" the needle replies.

She, ~~Tattoo~~ Artist

The pink elephant flaps away flies from her shoulder and whisks
around last night's reminiscence of booze and tar from her lips
and lungs. Or is it from this morning?

Flies scatter down her arm fading back into freckles flanked
by nicotine-flared veins—cliffs and ridges corner their escape. And
when asked, the spike pauses from striking the skin.

The constant hum from the gun is replaced by the hum of the A/C
machine. It was hard not to count the hard heart, heartbeat of water
drops dripping from the condensation line into a blue sand bucket
while she thinks. Drip-one.

Drip-two. Three. Drip-fifteen. The crows walk from her ears
to the windows of her eyes while she thinks about what to say. The
shop dresses like a punk band fronted by a country singer.

She spoke, "all you ~~hear~~ are the volumes of 'who's dick did you
suck to get this far?' I mean it's a very W░░░░ kind of thing,
especially among American Traditional tattooers."

She continues, "And females were commonly frowned
upon as being tattoo artists. There were a few in circus sideshows
as if they were the clowns throwing confetti from unicycles,
honking horns.

Men were the ringmasters. As a matter of fact Sailor Jerry was Ed
Hardy's teacher, Ed Hardy was Mike Malone's teacher, Mike
Malone is Keith Underwood's teacher, Keith Underwood…
is a part of the legacy.

But I digress. Back when Sailor Jerry was in Honolulu, Hawaii
he took in 'one.' Object. Thing. Nothing but in his first female
apprentice, and he had written to Ed, *I finally took a girl, long hair.
I took a fucking hippie in.*

And her fucking name is Kate." She reflects, "I think about Kate's
knots, have not's and haves, when I try to overcome my own ~~dick
sucking~~ issues.   And
Shanghai Kate stenciled herself as flash, permanent, inked
in our history

and on our flesh. We start as somebody's bitch for free. We draw.
We learn. We practice. We learn about sterilization, BBP, all shit
that people glass over when they watch those stupid reality tattoo
shows on TV.

And they are like, 'Oh, look. I want to be a tattooer. I want to buy
some kit on EBay and start fucking up my friends and giving
everybody hepatitis and staph.' She rants, 'Don't be a fucking
shitty scratcher. Nobody likes kitchen wizards.'"

Practice

Pay your dues.

She asks, "Do you see the bullet screaming for his life
on my forearm?" "One year we, my parents and I,
were in Rhinewhine, Germany and there's this guy getting a gun
tattoo outside in this little tent by a gazebo.

It wasn't a thing. I mean it was a thing, but it wasn't a thing. My
parents weren't covered or anything but they had a couple,
so it wasn't really a thing, but it was the first solid thing
I had as far as starting my own thing.

What you don't know is that both of my parents are military,
were military. My mom retired as a command sergeant major,
the highest-ranking female in the enlisted United States. My
dad retired as a first sergeant.

We had many pins in the map, rumbling from biker rally to latrines. So you see, I have hills, cliffs and ridges to climb. To prove. To earn. To be." She pauses. "I saw a halo encircling praying hands, and I walked into the tattoo shop.

I was every cliché. I was that girl. 'Oh my God, I want that!' At the last 15 minutes before they closed, I stared at some fucking random piece of flash on the wall. Panther. Star. Dagger. Skull. Cross. Rose. Praying hands was my first.

I paid like $180 for something that I would personally, now, normally would only charge, at most, like 120 bucks. But I earned it. I was the asshole then. The epitome of everything I can't stand now. But I mean it was mine, my baby steps in."

Step-one.

Step-two. Three.

Step-fifteen.

Dan's Interest

Until I can, I work customer service at █████████
and I spied a gentleman romping by with sleeves, ink
on his neck and face, on his legs, on his fingers,
and basically—painted.

During my break, I threw off my work shirt and
sleuthed this guy down. His appearance is best
described as gruff: long beard, dreaded, dark glasses,
silver ringed almost every finger, and about 55-
years-old. He lingered in the bargain cave, pawing
at fishing reels.

Dan:

*Excuse me sir. I noticed your tattoos and was wondering
if I could ask you some questions...*

Are you an artist?

Hank:

In the archives. Not anymore.

Dan:

Why did you stop?

Hank:

*Some days I humped from noon to five. No Prob.
But other days, I slumped over people until three AM.*

When someone comes in, you tattoo.

Dan:

Any advice for a novice?

Hank:

Draw.

to his story and then Amanda talking about the child they are raising, and how she talked about him I came to understand more of what it meant. I have seen Amanda plenty of times, but never saw her as happy as when Rob walked in. Clearly he is good to her.

I don't think I remember any girls lighting up like that when I showed up. A rough childhood in a bad area may have been his past. But he didn't let that drag him down or fall into the traps society has.

He is not the stereo type.

He got out.

He has a new life.

Rob stepped up and became a man taking care of his family and friends, got his life on track and moved out of the place that tried to consume him.

His artwork is large on his back covering most of the area, he is not sure if it's done just yet and wants to get a touch up but his artist was no longer working. One part he told me that the needles hit the spine area of his back didn't feel too good and made his nerves and fingers twitch. At one point during the session his whole arm sort of went limp and numb. The artist asked if he wanted to stop but he was like hell no not now keep going. In a way I hope that he leaves the ink on his back just as it is. I hope he never gets a touch up. After hearing his whole story taking notes and recording him I think it looks perfect.

The words Thug life were first on his back and are now starting to fade, the crosses are bold and easy to see. It looked right. His old life had faded away just as it was hard to read part of the thug life and his new faithful life was present and clear just like his triple cross is bold in his skin.

After dad Left her and Her mother
they were very Poor. no running
water in the house or heat in
winter. in Wisconsin winter.

Amanda grew up very fast.

* Mom tried to Keep them from
freezing to death on winter nights
By standing in Kitchen holding daughter
tightly in front of oven for warmth.
Said She remembers shivering. and
crying. Mom tried to a gas heater.
and was worried it would blow up.
mom told amanda If we Blew up
Mommy Loves you BABY. Amanda
had tears now...

16

Tattoo Artist

And it wasn't the rise but the fall
of my heart that led them to believe
I was gone.

And it wasn't until His air became mine
that I could become,
again.

And I continue to confess as if Ezekiel
is my preacher. In a way he is.

And I tell him that this tattoo defines my rebirth,
while the needle's vibrato plays over my
weeps and whispers.

And he says, "I'm stoked to do this, Man.
Sailor Jerry is my favorite style."

And a few weeks later I see Him,
again. He asks me how my tattoo is
doing.

And I say, "Healing. I am still
healing."

SECTION 44-34-10 (2)

'Tattoo facility' means any room, space, location, area, structure, or business, or any part of any of these places, where tattooing is practiced or where the business of tattooing is conducted.

The Irony of *Electric Relaxation* by A Tribe

Called Quest pulses a back/
drop. Pictures of ex/Notorious B-I-G, late/
Tupac, and Ol Dirty Bastard
(to name a few) shrine the walls.
This house is a base for hip
hop. And the hymn of the tattoo gun
forms as an honorary member to/
day. And the faintness of petroleum jelly
plays the role of audience a/
long with my calf. I lie on the ex/
massage table. For me, strength is wiped away
with my blood—by flimsy Brawny. And
we speak about Little Red Riding Hood.
Two stories emerge: 1) the one we all know.
Where Red, like Sherlock, unfolds
a mystery of Wolf and Grand/
mother, where big eyes and long nose
help her escape back home
through the woods. The message, of course,
is don't talk to strangers. 2) the one
we don't know, where Wolf
asks Red to strip and come
to bed. And she is eaten like pot
roast at the end. The linger of stew
potatoes and carrots puddle
on wood planks. Here,
she is victim. What is the moral
of this fairytale? I wonder.
These are the moments that I wonder
if my own strength will last as long
as this tattoo.

Tattoo Vs.

What has been witnessed,
heard, overheard, or sensed
a moment
an interaction,
a memory of flesh and violence

sacrifice

a mirror to the world,
God and shadow   our scars

Canvas or dartboard

a drunken star, a panther, barbed wire

flash stapled around the 90s,

Batman, Superman,
or the Incredible Hulk holding a burst of fire, Prometheus
an imitation of V.G's *Starry Night*
Andy Warhol's *Campbell's Soup Can,*
your spouse's first name,
                your last name,
your child's name,
or the name of your dead best friend encircling your right wrist,
dates
of the dead or
                        dates
of birth,   portraits of your mother,
your father,   your grandfather,
                                        your grandmother,
        your first cousin,   or Count Orlok
a puffer fish,
an octopus,
a squid, or
an angler fish

playing a twelve-string guitar,
a skull, a skull
and crossbones,
a skull
with a dagger
through it's arch,

                                                a heart,
                                        a heart
                                        and
crossbones, or   a heart
a dagger through its arch, its belly

A pirate SHIP,
a gypsy or pin up
a mermaid of your wife
flying through space,

a gargoyle, a gargoyle   crouching on the
earth, or
a gargoyle   hunched over a blank
gravestone,

                        a werewolf,
                        Little Red
                        Riding Hood
                        with the wolf
                        as a headdress,

a koi,
a dragon, or
a samurai soldier,
a bunny
a rabbit,
a hair
a fox, or

a duckbill platypus
   your daughter
      drew in third
          grade,
a butterfly,

rudiments and the US
9th Circuit, Redondo Beach.

   South Carolina against
   Ronald P. White. Prisoners

Me: Ok so I think the tattoo on your right arm is the one I want to focus on. ~~If you would please allow me to get a photo of it. Thank you. Alright so first question in the interview. Please describe your tattoo for me.~~

Don: That's what it looks like when I tattoo with my left hand.

Me: Uh, ok so you're an artist then?

Don: I was. I tattooed till about 1996 then I stopped.

Me: Why did you stop?

Don: ~~Didn't have enough time for it anymore. I had just had a daughter and I wanted to spend more time with her and my family and that's hard to do when you tattoo till odd hours in the morning.~~ *maybe keep* It's not like a normal job, some days you could be out of there by 11 but some days you won't make it home till 3 am. It's a demanding job, you can't just say I'm only going to stay for this long today. If someone comes in you tattoo them till it's done. ~~I own three shops still but I just own them, I let other people manage them.~~

Me: Awesome. So back to your arm, why did you tattoo that particular part of your arm?

Don: It's the only spot you can get with your left hand. Think about it, if you're using your left hand the only real places you can get are your right leg or right arm. If you're brave you could also do your stomach (he then lifted up his shirt to show me some words scribed across his belly).

Me: Is there any other meaning besides what it looks like to tattoo with your left hand?

Don: Well it started out as my right arm being my Vegas arm. One of my buddies tattooed most of the upper parts but I wanted to finish the last quarter of it.

Me: Alright, so how often do people ask you or say anything about your tattoo?

Don: Not often. I think most people are scared.

Me: Do you ever feel like you've been discriminated against because of your tattoos?

and pirates. Arizona
Supreme Court and explosions.

> Car chases cradling
> a cliff's edge. Two pistols

in your face. An asteroid screams
toward earth. Stubbed toes during

> a zombie apocalypse—
I've never seen a tattoo drip from a rotten
zombie. Can a wild "thing" that drifts between
> life and the after
boast praying hands on its shoulder?

What is forgotten
> is creation.

> Only death plagues the new world.

What makes us ~~in~~human is both death and creation—creativity
making new. When we lose the ability to create,

> we have already lost.

The more and more we delete creating,

> the more and more we delete humanity,

the more and more we become zombies.

> Undead. Dead?

> blood that stains like tattoos.

Beginning of

Cave drawing from

History of

Connection to

Types of

Philosophy of

Fine Art from

Marker of

Documentary Art of

Reception of

Literature about

Parker's Back and

Literature in

Performance of

Living art gallery over

Drama about

Ink Master to

Elements of

Public Art from

Techniques of

Pop Art from

Archive of

Clogged arteries in the Tin

Man. If he were hunched over
the padded edge and copper

top bar, would you approach him
and chat about aesthetics,

the theories of inter-
disciplinary approaches

to fine art?

Picasso and Pollack.
The cliché above her

ass; it weighs. Case No.
15 C 5891, 2015 WL 6501153.

Red Robin and Sam's Club.
Maricopa and Coleman.

Hermosa Beach and Key
West. Norfolk and Franklin

County. Copy machines.
Your reflection of

brush strokes and needle point. *One
man's vulgarity*: I have

two sleeves, split like bourbon

and milk, divided by

      a river of birth and death.
I am father. I am

"Diablo a Pié,"
a documentarian,

      a document. Selfish
      expression created by

duality: a canvas.
an artist. Skin my mother

      bore; it carries stains and masks,
      bold insecurities

and scrutiny—my tale
is open for inter-

      pretation. Now, my history
      is your history. And while

you may prescribe my story,

I ~~hold up~~ I am your mirror.

Knowledge hungry

Been told she was Illuminati
and satanist etc But aint.
* is deeply emotional. often
judged.

* real spiritual.
* thoughts on my Body
* dont trust people enough to
share
* make me happy.
Feel like I need an outlet!

Always happy with it.
Always new artist.
25 artists. not satisfied.
with work.
wants them redone.
Some touch ups.
wants aliens added to Back.
15 first tattoo.
2 the first time.
got six a year after.

"Passionate"
outlet
- hates the pain - angry -
survive the pain for the art
and expression.

* Binge tattooing *

29

Tattoo Parlor

I think there
are no great things
in the world anymore
until I see a neon sign's reflection
vibrate off the storefront window.
What a great thing. I think,
what a great thing to show
up blue and uninvited
then welcomed by the shimmer
of hope and glow,
hot and pink.

Foo Dog

He starts with a swift zee.
He lets the skin sip—

Zee
        Zee
Zee

before the gulp

Zee
        Zee

Zoooooo—

He wipes my arm as a mother
wipes a child's mouth full
of raspberry preserves.

And in between the ache,

he lifts the ink and blood.
The paper towel emulates my childhood,
A light blue comfort with frayed corners.
I gnaw the tips during dreams.

He dips the needle in water.
        In black.

He peels my skin

Zee
        Zee

Zoooooo

He settles into the eyes of the foo

dog on my arm.

He sees me for the first time
as the foo dog starts to see.

And you. All this time,
burning red, scared and angry,
didn't see the end.

Tattoo Gun

Imagine a 9mm bullet
clawing through sky and flesh,
fat and muscle,
bone and nucleus
at 820 mph. Devotion?

Perhaps the after-
burn of the barrel
rising against the temple
welcomes loyalty
      more than
scribing a crucifix on my back.

Why not call it a tattoo hammer
                    or drill?
Why not call it a spear
            of destiny?

Each are tools
for puncturing. Scribing
scars. Calligraphy. Both leave
beauty
to the eye of
the beholder.

B____

has Z_____ scratch *Gonzalez* cross his back. Bold
nasty, fat Old English while Dre's *Rat-Tat-*
Tat-Tat slaps the smoke back. Z_____ is faded.

Z_____ tats in fluorescents. His ink stacks shelves
behind the porcelain that B_____ laps on.
Blazing black and grays quick, Z____ is fire.

When Pops ran and Moms crashes to crack, B_____
steps up as man and is up to bat. He
cares for both hermanitos. Z_____ chisels stone.

As B_____ saddles the throne, Z_____ stands back, "You
good Mijo?" Z_____ shades most of the back, and
B_____ stays medium rare. Z_____ sizzles on.

The Burn

The tattoo shop vacated 26th street
and moved south to precinct line.
It abandoned the pool table and TV.
When asked why, it replied simply
with "TV gives you nothing
but a burnt tongue." Instead, the shop
plays a Sugarhill-like-hip-hop
like poured milk on jalapeños;
like A/C in a Texas summer;
like belated Daisies,
Stovers, and Hallmark;
the only thing that burned, now,
was my skin. I was getting a cross
on my bicep. A banner swung below,
waving my mother's name
to the world, at least, when I wear
sleeveless shirts she waves. Rita
may not have allowed tattoos in life,
but in death, she approves, I think.
I picture her leaning on her memories
inked in the clouds. Like a cliff
she leans over to look down on me
and smirk. I remember when I told her
that my girlfriend was pregnant. I thought
she would kill me. Yell at me.
Do something more than just say,
"pulling the cart before the horse,
aren't you?" And smirk. A four-
hour session is all I really can take.
I've heard of some of the shop's
clients sitting for eight hours
or more for one tattoo. I sit until
the burn is too much, the punctured
skin kills me. Yells at me. Does something
more.

Municipal Code § 17.06.070
September 12, 2007

They dismiss her claim
for lack of ripeness. They say—

No building shall be erected,
reconstructed, or structurally altered.
nor shall any building or land
be used for any purpose
except as hereinafter specifically provided
and allowed in the same zone
in which such building and land is located:

movie theaters,
restaurants,
adult businesses,
bars,
fortune tellers,
gun shops,
and youth hostels

No provision of the zoning code
permits tattooing

They use "tattooing" as shorthand—

Brianna described her tattoo as a teal infinity sign
with her brother's full name
written through it
on top of her left rib cage—

Her brother passed away

They said the act of tattooing

is not protected expression
under the First Amendment…

…it is not 'sufficiently imbued
with the elements of communication'

§ 7. TATTOOING.

The practice of tattooing is very common among criminals,
and is frequently carried to an extraordinary extent, twenty or
thirty
designs being occasionally found on the same subject. Lombroso
was the first
to point out the full biological and psychical significance of this
practice.

The Criminal
by Havelock Ellis

The wolf chose to enter her womb

and ~~People tattooed~~ tattooed people choose
to be the canvas. And though perceptions of
critics dressed in Granny's gown are slowly
eroding, just like many other things, change
is like stale bread—crunchy and scratchy—not
the better to eat you with.

Just Ink

      A woman's head tattooed on his right arm (memory of loss)
      A beginning of a name (record of love)
      A transfixed heart on his belly (to recall revenge)

The fewest are found among swindlers
and forgers, the most intelligent class
of criminals. These criminals refrain from
tattooing themselves because they know these
marks form recognition in the hands
of the police.

      Initials and daggers on his forearm (memory of revenges)
      Arrows on his thigh (record of love)
      A sun or the *camorra* on his hand (a great secret)

The greater are found among recidivists
and instinctive criminals—those who have committed
crimes against the person.

      The letters F and B on his right (her initials)
      The letters L and A on his left (his initials)
      A cross below his initials (bond with God)

Not sparing parts so sensitive as the sexual organs,
which are rarely touched even in extensive tattooing
among barbarous races, serves to show the deficient
sensibility of criminals to pain

      Two stars, one large, the other small on the left (hierarchy)
      An indistinct sign ending in a B near his wrist (forgotten
      love)
      A scar in left frontal region (will not say but suffers
      from giddiness).

Insensibility is observed by everyone familiar with prisons.

Black and Gray
10 years, intent to sell

I have it all over me—
shampoo and water mixed
with burnt carbon soot from newspaper
headlines. Once I tried to harvest the tar
from my lungs but they would not yield
to my addiction. Tattoos,
like heroin, cling forever.

But her name fades from my palm. Sara
is dying; her foot prints in the sand.

She's peppered between my fingers,
but it all just ends up failing, she fades
with time.

dealt with

inmates cut off tattoo for him

when deserve that tattoo

→ do we earn tattoos?

autobiography on skin

demon chained to the wall — addiction

prints of the past / Dream of the
future

Fear of hate
my shit

present ourselves to
curtis also eis

face tattoo —
f-you

Hate burned above lip

birth not 515   on right
iron cross   88

~~Smile Now, Cry Later~~
Cry Now, Smile Later

David, convicted
of assault—8 years

I rise against—
like every zombie film fronts—
to the Fall.

And, yet, I want
the piano wire, sharpened
by grit, to continue
to ache. To marrow.
And gnaw my flesh.
The ashes of newspaper
to creep and crawl as a virus.
A plague. Infect. The walking
dead.

Stick + poke

paper clips (skid sharp)
whenever I get a chance, I would
be hand poking on my holmies

black + gray   smile now
shady + fine lines

Inked by force
child murderer
("Katie's revenge")
on forehead

44

Department of Mystery

It is as if the surgeon drew a chalk
line with driftwood, fumbling between
faith and flesh. Each cut a split into
her nucleus, between discovery and destruction,
into her skin like prison bars—

> Prisoners must obey all rules,

> Prisoners must remain silent,

> Prisoners must not move.

He halved a butterfly. Now, her tattoo just
flutters wingless in a circle, split by a scar,
a brook, by her own body language.

And when she wakes
against the slumbering anesthesia,
it is as if she wanders into the walking dead, into
a post apocalyptic world, into *those who sleep
in death*, into the Fall—

> Prisoners must obey all rules,

> Prisoners must remain silent,

> Prisoners must not move.

And yet her eyes move before she can see.

Just Intonation

The more one is tattooed, he says,
the more one is esteemed and feared by comrades

Is that a moon or a flame that blends
into a saxophone, a blue note into
cold caffeine, sharp nights that whine and
cry for bars, or a beat that probes with
its index finger?

She was only 91713

*We have been baptized, we will carry
the tattoo on our left arm until we die*
—*Primo Levi*

Only a pile of skull, ribs, humorous,
and bones
wrapped in skin and sheeped in
to a pit.

Only a number un-
buried.

Only Rachel
was three-years-old.
Yes, three and then after—
three.

I am not just 111276

When it got hot, they dipped it into ink,
and burned it into my left arm, dot by dot
                                        —Eva Kor

I am not just un-

dead.

The numbers like embers

stoke white

hot cross stomach and forearm.

I was

If we bear all this suffering and if
there are still Jews left, when it is over
　　　　　　　　　　　　—Anne Frank

I was second, seconds
to last. I was branded, just a brand
and my existence erased—
my name, a list of names, burnt ash
into numbers and into ash, burnt
again.

right = lost love   left
tear drop outline — song to kill
          filled.   killed /attempt

convicted of assault — David

                   guitar string
                         ^
   needle barrel

                  sand paper to
                  sharpen
cup↓

    Nɩɩ can
    baby oil
Newspaper lunch bag over

     VO5 / water chapstick cap
     binding agent

      chess pieces
dry the ink / blends /

   Ryan | 6 years for
        arson

tattoos,   Prison Gang
X4 (XIV) northners   rules - code
SUTTA   Southerns (sur)
MS 13   XV3

michael   9/6 — hort
Tombstone = people killed
lips = kissed by gang
birth = ready to kill

walls
5 dots = history '¦'
prison

spider web — strand = prison time
clock no hands
drama masks

Demons

SS
⚡ — enforcer

I was like this / I will

11th gang

in house clean up
" That's how you earn tattoos —
at least — that's how you are supposed to

SECTION 44-34-10 (4)

'Tattoo or tattooing' means to indelibly mark or color the skin by subcutaneous
introduction of nontoxic dyes or pigments.

Monuments

Do you ever wonder the story
behind the abandoned house on some desert route?
About the rusty Ford that melts in the sand?
Its open doors? Its wanting?

Could it have been the gold that rushed in
life or the bones that quickened death? Which is greater,
the number of sand grains on earth or stars
in the sky? Was it some dreamer who stopped
and stared too long? At the sunset?
Lost in the horizon?

Do you ever wonder the what—
when tattoos pass by,
what truth they mask? What
does the skull and rose see
in you? The smile now
and cry later? Why does
the pinup salute? It's not
the walls. It's the man,
it's the scar.

Do you ever wonder the tale behind shades
of color? Why he shoulders an anchor, the
green smolders to blue.
Purple to gray.
Is it his fight from the war?
From the pain?

And his eyes draw in each time I ask.

And as the rust feeds the
desert floor, the tattoo eats
to skin and bone. And I am left
wondering.

What anchors you?

His tattoo basically is claiming and representing Communism. My interview person was claiming his beleif in "equal distribution between wealth and goods". He claims he loves his tattoo although it does cause controversary at times.

Father's First Tattoo
To Testicular Cancer

Where's Christ? He asks
as shade bleeds
into his skin. He already wants
the pink of his skin
to wash out the permanent,
waves wiping away sandcastles.

But as his flesh is marked
across his belly just below the button,
like the dots of Orion's belt where the devil rises.

Where's Christ, now? He asks.

I Ain't Your Daddy

Your mother played
the human pincushion
in a tattoo show—
echoed blood
beneath her acrylic nails.
She told me,
I wasn't the father.

Knowledge is the enemy
of faith, I replied

On Sunday,
You'll take the train
over to New Jersey.
What for? You ask.
What for?

sect. 4
- How we use them. / Why we use them.

We use tattoo's everyday in a form of art. It is how we express ourselves and talk without any communication. By looking at someones tattoo's you can determine their interest and what they like to do. They are also a level of identification and what they want to carry with them for the rest of their lives.

68

Most people today have permanent mascarea and lip makeup, another form of tattoos. They rather have their make up items tattooed on so they dont have to apply it everyday. If done professionally you could possibly save money on make up.

99

We use tattoo's to advertize social things such as nike, under amour, beer, etc. music, etc. Although sometimes they symbols were meant & the symbols wasnt they get the symbols because it is their interest, they are still advertising for that company. It is copy righted material,

34

temporary tattoo's also play a huge role in our society today. instead of getting one permantly they get one,

What Do Women Want

For Kim Addonizio

It is like
I am onstage with Madonna,
I am centerfold with Monroe,

But imagine I am on the back
of your book, spilling over your
shoulder, binging on your tattoos.

The bar swallows your voice and
        Good Girl trickles from my pen.

Tell me

       I trace black edges in the dark
       of *The Lovers*

Tell me

          I pierce
     traw skin of each letter—
     burn and scratch *Last Call*

Tell me

       If Depp took my wife
       What would be the odds
       we could devour each other's soul?

Tell her

Q. #3) if you don't mind me asking, who is she?

A. My cousin who passed away from cancer, Jennifer, she was very young, 28, she had a daughter who was 9 years old, and a few weeks before she passed away, her husband left her for his mistress. She was devastated. I credit him with her death, more than I do cancer. What an asshole.

Interviewer: He sounds like quite the douche bag. How could someone leave their wife, the mother of their daughter, on her death bed, for another woman? That's like a story for the record book.

Interviewee: *Oh yeah, for sure, my family has a shit ton of hatred towards him. He is a drug addict also, so his new girlfriend is not any role model for his young daughter. She (his mistress) has 4 other kids, by 4 other guys, and they aren't far apart in age, so you know she's a hoe... He dragged us through a custody case over my niece, oh, I totally left this part out, when my cousin was on her deathbed and he ran off with his mistress, he took their daughter with him, so she didn't get to say goodbye to her mom.*

silence for a few seconds

Q. #4) Did she get to go to the funeral?

A. *we basically had to threaten him to bring just her, because he was not allowed, he tried really hard to show his face, he was acting completely off the rocker, Jason, Jennifer's brother, was seriously about to damage him if he didn't calm down.*

Interviewer: *I would've beat the shit out of him, I'm sorry to be so blunt, but like, respect at a funeral, especially after what he did, just isn't optional. We could talk about this all day, but my*

Attach picture of

Christopher

color tattoo

here

if applicable

Fall

Yellowing leaves, like featureless men
and women, accuse each
other, point fingers at the other.
Blame her for letting go. Blame him
for not trying hard enough.

And as if the branches were its abacus,
the tree sums the fallen like echoes
of forgotten—their memories let go.
It lets go like the weathered initials
that were scarred into its bark
so many years ago. What happened
to D? What happened
to L?

1) Because the tattoo artist suggested a discount if her / her friend got the same tattoo in the same spot.

3) none was just going w/ a friend

4) yes, it got infected because she had to wear shoes / socks with it because it was winter (Infected 1week)

5) live life spontaneously

Anna's Addiction

The Eagle was a diamond ring to myself on my 21st
birthday. I stayed married for almost thirteen years,
and a tattoo was something, well, was something he
wouldn't have allowed. The artist voiced concern
about the scope of my first. He ask at least three times
as he drew, while he prepped, before he punished my skin.

I am sure.

The Swallow on my neck is a memorial—my grandmother.
She was the first I lost. She never trusted my ex. She
was a songbird, whistling warnings every once and awhile,
but of course I muted her song. That is, I never heard her
until she left me. I, now, will endlessly swallow her voice
with me.

I am sure.

My Rose on my foot was a piece of flash from the wall both
my "friend" and I chose. The artist offered us a discount. I think
he thought she was a snack. My husband thought she was a snack.
I am sure. Though we no longer talk, we are ~~linked~~ inked forever.
I don't wish badly on people, but I ~~sort of~~ smiled when I heard
hers became infected.

I am sure.

Unicorn Tattoo

I went to sleep, dreaming of being a unicorn
and woke a unicorn, dreaming of being a little girl.

I woke with no gold at the end of the rainbow;
no Santa Clause, Easter Bunny, or Tooth
fairy.

I used to want to be a magician, a wizard
that could bend space and time, leap amongst
the molecules of future and past.

I went to sleep, dreaming of flying, floating
down a staircase and woke with carpet fibers
between my toes.

I used to feel fantasies between pages of books,
within words. Now, I search and search endlessly
for leftover fragments of my childhood, the bread-
crumbs littering the forest path.

I used to want to be a unicorn. Now,
I just want to be treated like one.

Interview
1. its a hypnotised robot holding a bouquet of mushrooms
2. Two years ago in Detroit Michigan
what made you get this particular tattoo
my love fer electronic music and the
fact that something that doesn't have life
5 holding something that has life. Love
hipntizes you

3. This __ a robot holding a flower
— why did you want that ... what made
you want this
hold on__, I was stoned. I was high
on illegal grade medical mariquen. Dude
4. like was it what you invisioned?
yes. the artist knew I wanted the
psychocllictnice. tripiness of it.
Did you know the tattoo artist.
no.
why did you let him do it
I was in a state I've never been in
Did you just walk in off the street.
no.. I just made an appointment
How did you hear about that place if your from texas?
a friend of mine had worked there
did you plan the tatt here?
yes
& then why Michigan..!
I went up thore w/a friend and
heard they have good ink
long did you think about this tattoo before getting
it.
2 years
x anything influencey you to get this tattoo?
corrupt robots
wtt abut them
how corrupt society seems to take over the
world and one day robots will talk over the world

66

Confessional

I crave it there. Kind of
stupid, but I'm a huge Hello
Kitty fan and it landed on my hip
to fit my body type.

                 To fit my faith.

To hide it for dance.

                 To fit my faith
it kisses my fleshy spandex.

My original thought was my wrist
with it's name forming an infinity sign,

                 but infinity is forever.

It's a reminder of autonomy
and nonconformity—a representation
of what I feel. I saw it on the wall
of the tattoo parlor.

I was eighteen, and If I could do it over,
you know, I would get

a memorial to honor my son
who was never born.

1 round pointy cross w/ pink
heart (♡) in the center
2. personal reasons concerning my
faith on my hip bone
3 original idea was just a plain
cross, talked me into getting one
that goes with my body type.
4. No, it came out exactly how
they described it
5 the meaning is that God comes
first & I believe in his word with
all my heart.
6 N/A
7 Not very often actually
8. A lot ask why I got it in
that place specifically.
9 No the only people who've seen
it are my friends & family &
they all love it.

She captures a ladybug

only to let it go;
it cannot be contained. She asks, "Will it find true love?"
She points to the moon, "La Luna!" And reaches. She sees
gravity lassoing the earth and my arms
holding her, resisting the fall
toward the heavens. "Your arms are the sky,
Daddy." She says. "Did it burn when they painted
the Sun on your arm?" She circles my tattoo
as if it is the center of her world.

light Brown, red, black__stitching
bear   irratation

1. A teddy bear with stitches and a pin going through the heart

2. Next available space on arm.

3. To get a bear that represents his friend in Iraq in the Marines with Hern. Sniper hit him in the helmet and shrapnel hit in face, so stitches on cheek and horns on head. Hern turned mean.

4. No, it darkened and looks how you want.

5. Remembering friendship that's past

6. Body Temple tatoo in ocean side California. Drew it himself. worked there as piercer. Boss applied.

7. Family flack. Now they're used to it. Friends didn't ask meaning.

8. Demonic teddy bear.

9. shows off tattoos

10. erased old (1st tatoo) to start over

Scars Over Water

The first tattoo I knew leapt from my step-grandfather,
an anchor encircled by a serpent. Perhaps the rod of God
stained his forearm. Could it split seas like it divided family?
By the time I saw his tattoo, as a young boy, age and sun
muted it green like algae creeps on the edge of a rock. You
know the old cliché, "if walls could talk?" Well, the same
could be said of his tattoo. It may have been etched with ink
during his stent in the navy, but it didn't scar until he over-
looked, an overlord over waters, and it didn't heal until after
he died.

Every year we vacationed at the beach house. His room jettied,
out as if into the ocean, as if a Viking prow pierced through
the spirits of the gods. It shadowed the sand, forming his identity.
And as Ellison said, *Shadows are the source of identity.*

I'm not sure what the anchor and serpent symbolized
for my grandfather—his longing for the ocean, his remembrance
of sailing, battle, war, or just the smoke lifting from the ship's
stack. Maybe it represents the discoveries
he never wanted to discover, sins that history books and bibles
only whisper at. He did, however, use it as an entrance the same
as the Tornado whirled Dorothy into Oz. There, in a dream world,
she discovers reality and truth. And the Lion growls out courage,
the Scarecrow remembers his brain, and the Tin Man beats
with a heart. The same could be said for my grandfather. When we
vacation, there, he uncovers his truth, buried behind the pocket
door of his room, the untold secrets that lie within his
grandchildren.
There, the reality felt like the dream world—the tattoo shadowed
our shoulders and unspoken promises were broken.

I always wondered, though, if it was the serpent that strangled
the anchor or was the anchor drowning the serpent.

I Sail My Fingers

down the red river from the mouth of his
throat to just below his chest. His scar, a memory
of humanity, an actuality of his. I pretend a crab
tries to anchor its claws to the outer banks
as the flow, the rapids rush it hopeless; it reaches
for rock, branch, or flesh, though ever drifts farther
away. And further down. And it cobbles
over the thousands of blue, yellow, and green reeds,
which sift through the sand and pebble beneath
the river's roar. These are his connectors, his veins that once
interviewed and interlocked his heart with his lungs,
to his soul. If this crab—   if I could
just grasp and control these leads to life, try to
bring him from the depths, try, as well, to save myself…

                                 I doubt
he knows rivers as Hughes knew rivers, but he heard
a splash and wake. And he may be, now, speaking of rivers
with Hughes and others. And though He witnessed a human
inevitability, perhaps, just possibly, this scar is, instead,
the beginning, a rough outline, his rendering of the Colorado,
the Rio Grande, or just the aqueduct through California.
Just maybe it's his story, a symbol
to be.

ACKNOWLEDGMENTS

Some poems contained in this book originally appeared in the following journals:

Tempered Runes Press—   The Irony of *Electric Relaxation* by A Tribe

Solum Literary Press—   Scars Over Water

Monuments

Department of Mystery

Fall

Tattoo Parlor

Beyond Words—   Unicorn Tattoo

Wingless Dreamer—   She captures a ladybug

Subprimal Poetry Art—   I Sail My Fingers

Carbon Culture—   I Tell Them Ink is Mightier Than Pen and Sword

Amarillo Bay—   The Burn

Tattoo Highway—   Diego

BOOKS BY DONOVAN HUFNAGLE

Sunshine Special

Shoebox

30 Days of 19

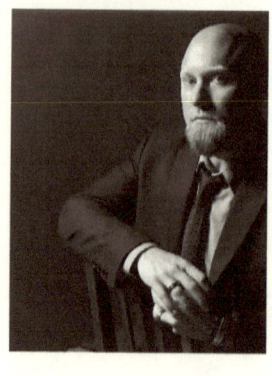

Donovan Hufnagle is a husband, a father of three, and a professor of English and Humanities. He moved from Southern California to Prescott, Arizona to Fort Worth, Texas. He has three poetry collections: *The Sunshine Special* is "part personal narrative, epic poem, and historical artifact;" *Shoebox* is based on true events and is an epistolary, poetic narrative about Juliana's "past and present, love and lack, in language that startles;" and *30 Days of 19* uses inverted Haiku poems juxtaposed to Trump tweets, capturing the first thirty days of the Covid 19 quarantine. Other recent writings have appeared in *Tempered Runes Press, Solum Literary Press, Poetry Box, Beyond Words, Wingless Dreamer, Subprimal Poetry Art, Americana Popular Culture Magazine, Shufpoetry, Kitty Litter Press, Carbon Culture, Amarillo Bay, Borderlands, Tattoo Highway, The New York Quarterly, Rougarou*, and others.

ENDORSEMENTS

In poetry that draws on memoir, interviews, customer questionnaires, Havelock Ellis, descriptions of prison tats, and local legal codes, Donovan Hufnagle shows us how tattoos are life stories in the flesh. Using language that is always interesting, even astounding, he demonstrates the ways tattoos function as metaphor and metonym: we want to make our plans indelible, later to find them in need of revision, deletion, or acceptance.

—Joseph Harrington, author of Of Some Sky and Things Come On (an amneoir)

There is nothing more intimate than skin. In this way, Donovan Hufnagle's latest poetry collection is staggeringly intimate. In it we find ourselves rifling through the back-office desk in the tattoo parlor, uncovering the story of skin in the artifacts, scraps, and half-thoughts we find there. *Raw* is a mythic space of tattoos, artists, and their stories. A tattoo-artist narrator in one poem tells us the secret he's keeping from the girl considering the dragonfly tattoo, that "ink cuts away your flesh. I cut and burn you." In this strikingly intimate space, we discover a truth only poetry can tell. The truth is that this will fuck us up, it will hurt, and we will be scarred for life. Like ink that tunnels through flesh, Hufnagle's poems leave channels in the mind. Rivers of truth that allow us to consider the nature of skin, and pain, and the desire underneath it all.

—Susan Ayotte Norman, author of *26 Queens*

Donovan Hufnagle has assembled a careful poetic ethnography of tattooed bodies and the stories that they tell. Just as the tattoo inscribes meaning on the body, this book elegantly reveals the stories that only the body can tell. It is a book that connects tattoo adorned bodies to a profound human truth: we are each other's mirrors, and the artful inscriptions of our bodies connect us to each other in ways that transcend political and social divides. This is an urgent book that does what only the best poetry can do; it opens spaces for conversation, connection, and healing.

—Kristin Prevallet, author of I, Afterlife: Essay in Mourning Time.